Elliott Carter

Retracing II

for Horn in F

HENDON MUSIC

DISTRIBUTED BY

7777 W. BLUEMOUND RD. P.O. BOX 13819 MILWAUKEE, WI 53213

www.boosey.com
www.halleonard.com

Published by Hendon Music, Inc.
a Boosey & Hawkes company
229 West 28th Street, 11th Floor
New York NY 10001

www.boosey.com

AN IMAGEM COMPANY

ISMN 979-0-051-10689-9

First printed August 20, 2009

Music engraving by Robert Nowak

HORN in F

RETRACING II

Elliott Carter

12 June 2009 NYC

Printed 20 August 2009